From Risk
to Reason

S&F

SF Communications of Georgia
P.O. Box 1311
Clarkesville, Georgia 30523

To contact the authors:

Dick Stafford
email: staff1@windstream.net
dickstafford@windstream.net
1-706-499-3914

Mike Fitsko
63 Hunters Point
New Braunfels, Texas 752
1-800-585-5475
email: mfitsko@satx.rr.com

1 2 3 4 5 6 7 8 9 0

ISBN # 978-0-96504-784-5
Printed and distributed in the US by Lightning Source, Inc.
Cover design by DID Media, Cornelia, Georgia 30531

US $12.95

From Risk to Reason

100 Reasons
to Vote for
Changing America
in 2008

by
FITSKO & STAFFORD

The authors chose to write this book
in the fall of 2007 in a place
symbolic of our country's
lack of effective leadership
these past seven years:
NEW ORLEANS.

PREFACE

Our culture has confidently embraced the concept of risk from business to friendships. We see it as necessary to expand corporate opportunities, develop new relationships and encourage growth. Risk is as fundamental to our society as American apple pie. But unnecssary risk can be destructive. Within the global communuty it can cause wars, destroy innocent lives and waste billions of dollars. More importantly, needlesss risk diverts attention and energy from the real crises on our planet to fabricated ones. Our collection of original quotations is an attempt to recognize what has gone wrong the last seven years and why we should use reason in making decisions about the reality in which we now live. We hope our thoughts will encourage discourse and thought for the presidential election of 2008. It is a critical moment for America and Americans.

You don't make
America
GREAT
by making the
American people
small.

"Stay the course"
is a tragedy...
not a strategy!

Because
winning the peace
is as critical as
winning the War.

"All of us have to recognize
that we owe our children more than
we have been giving them."

— **HILLARY CLINTON**
Candidate for President

Being patriotic doesn't include *exterminating* liberty.

You find hypocrisy
dishonest
and
distasteful.

When given the option, you prefer a *surge* of intelligence... and *not* a surge of stupidity.

Because a country
deserves a leader who
lives in the present,
recognizes reality and
refuses to *veto*
the future.

"We should not let the actions
of terrorists cause us to
reject our American system of justice.
The ultimate terror
in a democracy is the destruction
of constitutional powers."

DENNIS KUCINICH
Candidate for President

The American Dream does not include a vow of poverty.

Actively searching for peace is *not* a sign of weakness...
but a
badge of courage.

To find a cure for
the disease
that killed
Republican President
Ronald Reagan.

You believe that in
America *everyone*
deserves a chance
to sit at the
table of opportunity.

Intelligence should
never be confused
with vast, wandering
and pointless cliches.

You much prefer your
Supreme Court
justices sit up straight,
rather than leaning
too far
to the right.

Exploiting
fear
to run government
disappeared with
monarchies.

"I don't oppose all wars.
What I am opposed to is a dumb war.
What I am opposed to is a rash war."

— **BARACK OBAMA**
Candidate for President

The cost of the
War on Terror
should not include
the
Bill of Rights.

You believe *torture* is as un-American as Communism and Fascism.

The 18th Century
King George
and
our 21st Century
King George
haven't been good
for America.

You prefer the
name of
CIA undercover
operatives
be kept *well*
undercover.

"Raising a family is difficult enough. But it's even more difficult for single parents struggling to make ends meet. They don't need more obstacles. They need more opportunities".

— **BILL RICHARDSON**
Candidate for President

You are picky
about which
lies
to believe.

Because New Orleans matters.

So that
The Constitution
can be retrieved from
Karl Rove's
office trash can.

So that
"Mission Accomplished"
can finally
be accomplished.

"I choose bold. I choose action.
I choose what's right for
the people. I choose to
make a difference."

— **BILL RICHARDSON**
Candidate for President

The vision
that *is* America
should not
be overshadowed
by a
censorship
of the truth.

"The very institutions we need to build to have us effectively engage and fight back against terrorism; this administration seems to take the other track and move in another direction. We need leadership that knows how to engage participation."

CHRISTOPHER DODD
Candidate for President

Because you believe
only oceans
should separate
America from the rest
of the world...
not unbridled
beligerence.

Fitsko & Stafford

"You're doing a heckuva job, Brownie."

Homeland security *doesn't* mean homeland imprisonment.

To move Haliburton's office out of the White House.

It's easy to block promising stem cell research when you are hostile to reason and knowledge.

"It costs money to have universal health care. It's not cheap, but I'd pay for it by getting rid of Bush's tax cuts for people who make over $200,000 a year."

— **JOHN EDWARDS**
Candidate for President

So the
White House
will be held
accountable for...
its actions,
its rhetoric and
its policies.

Democrats know how
to pronounce
"nuclear."

You honestly believe
that wiretapping
without a warrant
is illegal.

You understand the concept of, "Keeping your friends close and your enemies closer," and more importantly...

you know the difference.

Removing
Saddam Hussein
didn't make
America safer...
but removing
Republicans will.

"Let me tell you. There's only
one thing worse than a
soldier dying in vain, it's
MORE soldiers dying in vain."

MIKE GRAVEL
Candidate for President

Think how mad you'll make Bill O'Reilly...

...and
Rush Limbaugh.

How else will the
Dixie Chicks
ever get to perform
at the
White House?

Just in case
Tom Delay
decides to run again.

You believe the
Supreme Court
should make
decisions that
support our
Constitutional
freedoms.

"There is not a liberal America and a conservative America — there is the United States of America. There is not a black America and a white America and a Latino America and Asian America… there's the United States of America."

— BARACK OBAMA
Candidate for President

You're sick of
pasty-faced white
guys all wearing
the same
suit and tie.

When you dig
really deep into
what Republicans
truly believe,
you discover
they're really
quite shallow.

You've heard rumors
that
Ann Coulter
is going to vote
Republican.

FITSKO & STAFFORD

FOX NEWS.
Need we say more?

Republicans
love war
and
hate sex.

"Education enables people and societies to be what they can be. It is education that allows us to see that we are in this for the long haul, and it is education that will give us the tools we need to build a better future."

—BILL RICHARDSON
Candidate for President

You want an economy with less inequality and more opportunity for over-worked and overlooked middle class Americans.

You believe all children deserve quality, low-cost health care.

Karl Rove's gone. Why not the rest of them?

Your grandchildren
are counting on you to
clear up the mess the
Republicans
have made the past
eight years.

Make that eight years of messes.

"My parents shared not only an improbable love, they shared an abiding faith in the possibilities of this nation. They would give me an African name, Barack, or blessed, believing that in a tolerant America your name is no barrier to success."

— BARACK OBAMA
Candidate for President

Government should serve the people... not the other way around.

You know America's
best days didn't
end with
Ronald Reagan.

You understand
one's
sexual orientation
doesn't define
a person's character.

Tax cuts for the rich
aren't in your
top 10
when it comes to
urgent problems
facing America.

When it comes to
people,
you're not a
"compassionate
conservative,"
you're just
compassionate!

"The challenges of change are always hard. It is important that we begin to unpack those challenges that confront this nation and realize that we each have a role that requires us to change and become more responsible for shaping our own future."

— **HILLARY CLINTON**
Candidate for President

You want to make
certain Orwell's
1984
remains a work
of fiction.

Wounded war heroes deserve better than Walter Reed.

G.O.P.
really means that
<u>G</u>ay, <u>O</u>ld or <u>P</u>oor
need *not* apply.

To ensure future
generations
understand the truth
about the
Bush legacy:
one disaster
after another.

Because
"Freedom Fries"
is a slogan...
not a plan.

"Ignorance has always been the weapon of tyrants; enlightenment the salvation of the free."

— **BILL RICHARDSON**
Candidate for President

You believe the
government should
solve problems,
not create
diversions like
flag burning...

FITSKO & STAFFORD

and Terri Shivo.

You truly care
about the lives
of the
less fortunate.

You believe in America's promise...

...and the American Dream.

"Today we are engaged in a deadly global struggle for those who would intimidate, torture, and murder people for exercising the most basic freedoms. If we are to win this struggle and spread those freedoms, we must keep our own moral compass pointed in a true direction."

BARACK OBAMA
Candidate for President

You were taught
in high school and
still believe that
there are three
distinct and separate
branches of
government.

You don't think
television preachers
should set
America's agenda.

Because you believe
church and state
are not the same
thing...
thank God!

You believe
oil companies are
rich enough to be
held accountable...
and *not* just to their
rich friends.

Your definition of a free society includes your Right to Dissent.

"Whether you are a Democrat or a Republican, our nation is stronger when we are respected throughout the world."

BILL RICHARDSON
Candidate for President

Governing requires
much more than just
getting elected,
even if you are
not elected by the
majority.

You're tired of the "Party of whatever works."

Over 3,875
American deaths
in Iraq
and counting...

...and over 30,000 injured Americans in Iraq.

———————

(fill in the number)
deaths of *innocent*
Iraqi men, women
and children
in Iraq.

"The very institutions we need to build to have us effectively engage and fight back against terrorism; this administration seems to take the other track and move in another direction. We need leadership that knows how to engage participation."

— **CHRISTOPHER DODD**
Candidate for President

You believe "Cowboy Diplomacy" should have *remained* in the Old West.

Moe, Larry, Curly...
Rudy, Mitt, Fred:
same difference.

Republican Strategy

...isn't that an oxymoron?

Does
Abu Ghraib
ring a bell?

After eight years, isn't it time for competence?

"Focusing your life solely on making a buck shows a certain poverty of ambition. It asks too little of yourself. Because it's only when you hitch your wagon to something larger than yourself that you realize your true potential."

BARACK OBAMA
Candidate for President

Republican competence.

...isn't that another oxymoron?

You don't just preach
family values
...you *practice* them!

FITSKO & STAFFORD

You appreciate the
difference between
vice and virtue...
unlike some
Congressmen.

When it comes to
public schools,
you prefer religion
not be one of the
3 R's.

You fail to
understand the
concept of

"No rich, white child
left behind."

"What we have to do... is to find a way to celebrate our diversity and debate our differences without fracturing our communities."

— **HILLARY CLINTON**
Candidate for President

To fill the
ever-widening gap
between the
promise
and the
delivery.

Given the choice,
you prefer to
raise taxes
than
raise debt.

Harriet Myers still has her eye on the Supreme Court.

You simply
refuse to trust
a multi-married guy
whose first name is
"Newt."

You like reading
books by authors
other than
Ann Coulter
and
William Bennett.

You realize
Rush Limbaugh
is a comedian,
but you don't find
him *particularly*
funny.

"It is my view that we cannot
conduct foreign policy
at the extremes."

— **JOE BIDEN**
Candidate for President

Because you believe
one of the BEST
ways to
support our troops
is with a first class
U.S. Veterans
Health Care System.

Because you don't
trust politicians who
swagger...
especially while
sitting down.

Truthfulness,
integrity and
accountability
have always been
important to you.

A President's ego should at least be proportionate to his brain.

To build a more tolerant America.

To elect a President
who is
ready to lead
America
the morning after
his inauguration.

"The challenge is to practice politics as the art of making what appears to be impossible, possible."

— **HILLARY CLINTON**
Candidate for President

To create
a world where
"No citizen is
left behind."

To restore America's standing in the global community.

To remove chaos
from Iraq and build
peaceful lives
for those who live
there.

To provide an
honorable and just
way immigrants and
their families can
join our
workforce legally.

So that we can begin
to live
without **fear**
and
with **hope**.

So the
United States
Justice Department
can work daily...
truly *seeking*
justice for all.

"We must become energy-independent because it affects our national security."

— **BILL RICHARDSON**
Candidate for President

To help
make it possible
to shift spending
$10 million a day
from war...
to peace.

To cut the strings
between
government officials
and oil companies
so that we might truly
seek alternative fuels
to benefit
all Americans.

You believe
Swift Boats
should remain in
water...
not politics.

Isn't it about time we
address the issue of
climate change?

...before it's too late.

Of all people, the
Vice President of the
United States
should respect both
The Constitution
...and perhaps the
Code of Conduct
for hunters.

You prefer
government that
keeps its check book
balanced...

not $9 trillion in
the RED.

"He tried to kill my Daddy," is NOT a good enough reason to invade a sovereign country.

A *smart* son should READ and FOLLOW his own father's advice:

"Trying to eliminate Saddam would have incurred incalculable human and political costs. We would have been forced to occupy and control Baghdad and rule Iraq. There was no viable exit strategy."

— George Herbert Walker Bush
A World Transformed, 1998

You prefer
government leaders
who actually
fulfill their military
service commitment,
rather than
spending their time
campaigning
for friends
while on duty.

FITSKO & STAFFORD

The Republican tax cuts are as "Fair and Balanced" as FOX News.

Because you believe a family of four with an above-average salary, working three jobs and involved in the community, should NOT face foreclosure of their home mortgage.

You prefer a leader
who understands
that the word
COALITION
means
more than one.

Even if you ARE enthralled while reading *My Pet Goat* while the country is under attack, a good leader knows when it's time to sit up, say 'Excuse me,' and leave the room.

"I have political capital and I intend to spend it!"

On what?

More blood for oil?

Americans may be
addicted to oil,
but they are also
addicted to sound,
competent
leadership.

The *only* weapon
of mass destruction
found in the last
seven years is the
Republicans'
choice of
POWER
over
PRINCIPLE!

You believe the
U.S. Attorney
General should be
loyal FIRST to the
American people and
The Constitution
and secondly to the
President...
NOT the other way
around.

Isn't it time
we stopped making
American *ill will*
our number one
export?

When it comes
to political
appointments,
you don't believe
competence
should be
compromised.

You readily
understand that,
in war, old soldiers
may never die...
but lots of
young ones
do!

You've grown
weary of the
deep divisions
that have been
created
by the great
"Uniter."

You believe that being the "decider" means you expect a leader to weigh ALL the possibilites in any given situation, especially war... before actually *deciding*.

You understand that
freedom isn't free,
but neither
should it be
for sale
to the highest
bidder.

Enough
is
enough!

PRESIDENTIAL PRIMARY DATES

Presidential Primary
Iowa
January 2008

Presidential Primary
Wyoming
January 2008

Presidential Primary
New Hampshire
January 2008

Presidential Primary
District of Columbia
January 2008

Presidential Primary
Michigan
January 2008

Presidential Primary
Nevada
January 2008

Presidential Primary
Florida
January 2008

Presidential Primary
South Carolina
January 2008

Presidential Primary
Alabama
February 2008

Republican Caucus
Maine
February 2008

Presidential Primary
Arizona
February 2008

Presidential Primary
Arkansas
February 2008

Presidential Primary
California
February 2008

Presidential Primary
Connecticut
February 2008

Presidential Primary
Delaware
February 2008

Presidential Primary
Georgia
February 2008

Presidential Primary
Illinois
February 2008

Presidential Primary
Missouri
February 2008

Presidential Primary
New Jersey
February 2008

Presidential Primary
New Mexico
February 2008

Presidential Primary
New York
February 2008

Presidential Primary
Oklahoma
February 2008

Presidential Primary
Rhode Island
February 2008

Presidential Primary
Tennessee
February 2008

Presidential Primary
Utah
February 2008

Presidential Primary
Louisiana
February 2008

Presidential Primary
Virginia
February 2008

Presidential Primary
Washington
February 2008

Presidential Primary
Wisconsin
February 2008

Presidential Primary
Massachusetts
March 2008

Presidential Primary
Ohio
March 2008

Presidential Primary
Texas
March 2008

Presidential Primary
Vermont
March 2008

State Primary
Puerto Rico
March 2008

Presidential Primary
Mississippi
March 2008

Presidential Primary
Pennsylvania
April 2008

Presidential Primary
Indiana
May 2008

Presidential Primary
North Carolina
May 2008

Presidential Primary
Nebraska
May 2008

Presidential Primary
West Virginia
May 2008

Presidential Primary
Kentucky
May 2008

Presidential Primary
Oregon
May 2008

Presidential Primary
Idaho
May 2008

Presidential Primary
Montana
June 2008

Presidential Primary
South Dakota
June 2008

State Primary
Maine
June 2008

State Primary
North Dakota
June 2008

State Primary
Virgin Islands
September 2008

State Primary
Kansas
August 2008

State Primary
Guam
September 2008

State Primary
Colorado
August 2008

State Primary
Minnesota
September 2008

State Primary
Alaska
August 2008

State Primary
Hawaii
September 2008

ABOUT THE AUTHORS

MIKE FITSKO is a retired educator, freelance writer and moti-
vational speaker. He has served as an English and history teacher,
Dean of Students, a middle and high school principal as well as
Assistant Superintendent for Curriculum and Instruction. He con-
tinues to write, lecture, and present management seminars to schools
and corporations around the country. For the past eight years, he has
written a popular weekly newspaper column for the New Braunfels,
Texas *Herald-Zeitung* and works part time as a student specialist for
San Antonio College. The winner of numerous awards and recogni-
tions, Mr. Fitsko resides in south central Texas with his wife of 29
years, Debbie.

RICHARD STAFFORD is a teacher, college professor, writer and
public speaker living in the Southeast. He has taught middle school,
high school and traditional/non-traditional college and university
students for almost thirty years. He is also the author of six books of
fiction and non-fiction, four stage plays and three musicals. Stafford
has written over a hundred magazine and periodical articles includ-
ing interviews with Arthur Miller, Edward Albee and *New York Times*
editor, Frank Rich. His teaching awards include the Delta Gamma
Professor of the Year, Sears Foundation Campus Leadership and
Education Excellence Award, and Teacher of the Year award in
three institutions. He is married to a school administrator, Kristal,
and has two sons in college. He is an avid hiker, sailor, enjoys gar-
dening and traveling througout the world.